ISBN 9781906276980

Cover *Day of Rest Lobuje*

Photo by Unknown

To Hilary Hall.
Best wishes,
Eileen H...
30-7-18

CONTENTS

f. Day 7. FRIDAY APRIL 8 1977
KHARTE/overKHARTE
PASS/CHANDRIKARKA
10,300 feet (7 hours approx)

g. Day 8. SATURDAY APRIL 9 1977
CHANDRIKARKA/JORSALE   9,000   feet
(approx 6 hours)

h. Day 9. SUNDAY APRIL 10 1977
JORSALE /NAMCHE BAZAAR 9,200 feet
(3 hours approx)

i. Day 10. MONDAY APRIL 11 1977
NAMCHE BAZAAR/TENBOCHE
12,715 feet (5 ½ hours approx)

j. Day 11. TUESDAY APRIL 12 1977
TENGBOCHE (Day of rest)

k. Day 12. WEDNESDAY APRIL 13 1977

l. Day 13. THURSDAY APRIL 14 1977
DINGBOCHE (Day of rest)

m. Day 14. FRIDAY APRIL 15 1977
DINGBOCHE/LOBUJE 16,175 feet (5
hours approx)

n. Day 15. SATURDAY APRIL 16 1977
LOBUJE (Day of rest)

o. Day 16. SUNDAY APRIL 17 1977
LOBUJE/GORAKSHEP-KALAPATAR
18,175 feet (3 hours approx)

p. Day 17. MONDAY APRIL 18 1977
LOBUJE/PANGBOCHE 13,000 feet (7
hours approx)

q. Day 18. TUESDAY APRIL 19 1977
PANGBOCHE/SYANGBOCH 13,000
feet (6 hours approx)

r. Day 19. WEDNESDAY APRIL 20 1977
SYANGBOCHE/KATHMANDU via LUKLA

3. Epilogue

4. Suggested Packing List

Introduction

High over the Himalaya in the kingdom of Nepal I sat in our tiny aircraft which was taking us to the starting point of our Everest trek. Gazing down on the icy wastes of endless mountains I was suddenly touched by panic. Was I really fit enough to make this arduous trip? It was a bit late to change my mind. I had reached the point of no return. It was now or never.

For years I had dreamed of Everest, following in the footsteps of the legendary climbers, Hillary and Bonington. I searched the libraries and bookshops for information until I knew the route backwards. There was no internet in the 1970s.

I had thought about it long enough so I decided it was now or never. At 41, I could not afford to wait any longer so I booked my place on a trek with an excellent tour operator Bales Worldwide

Tours, a family company who were well respected in the travel trade.

I was faced with two problems, I had to find the money and at the same time attain some degree of fitness. My walking experience was limited and this was not exactly a stroll in the Surrey hills.

Fortunately there was plenty of overtime in my job at BT so I cashed up my last insurance policy. Forget about old age, that's in the future. Better to spend the money now. I left the car at home and cycled the 17 miles return trip to work at least four times a week. The 11 flights of stairs in my office block became my lunchtime training ground.

In January I had a setback. A bad attack of bronchitis left me with an asthmatic problem. My friends advised me not to go. They didn't think I was fit enough. I in turn assured them that I was perfectly all right and the altitude would either kill or cure me. Privately, I had my reservations but armed with a pile of pills to cope with every eventuality, I decided come what may I was going.

So now read on. This diary gives a detailed account of my journey in 1977 and how it was before mass trekking became the norm. At first the tourists came in a trickle, but in the 60s and 70s the groups began to escalate, although there was little evidence of it on our trek except for the litter at some of the camp sites. The route now heaves with tourists. There are even queues and grid lock at some of the stops. Lodges have been built to provide more comfort for the trekker. Camping is no longer the norm. There have been many changes along this route including an increase in theft with the influx of foreigners, unheard of in the 70s; there are very few violent crimes committed and the Khumbu region is still one of the safest areas in Nepal.

Decades have passed since my trek to Everest but as I look back I realize that it still remains the ultimate in adventure and one of the highlights of my life. An experience of mind and body that has lasted a lifetime. There has been nothing to equal it. At the end of my account I have included a packing list, also details of a few of the birds in the Everest regions and some handy hints on etiquette just in case you want to 'Follow in My Footsteps.'

Swayambunath Kathmandu

My Diary
Days 1. and 2.
SATURDAY and SUNDAY APRIL 2 and 3 1977
KATHMANDU Sightseeing 5000 feet

We had arrived in Kathmandu to a chaotic airport with cattle on the runway. Soon we were settled into our hotel where we were advised that our trek was leaving one day early and to make sure we packed all essentials in our rucksack as our kitbags may be a day late. In my case this means as much as I can get into my rucksack and as much as I can wear comfortably. I take these Nepalese days with a pinch of salt.

Kathmandu the only major city in Nepal, is full of exciting diversions and I was out of bed long before breakfast, desperate to see the sights. The place was buzzing; everywhere there was colour and excitement. I saw porters carrying fruit and vegetables to the market and men and women offering gifts of flowers and offerings of food to the many shrines and temples dedicated to the complex system of the Hindu gods.

Then back to the hotel in time for breakfast which turned out to be boiled eggs. The salt was damp. When I opened the salt cellar I saw rat droppings. I wondered how many more surprises like this we would find during our journey.

We spent the rest of the day sightseeing in the Kathmandu valley, visiting the Buddhist *stupas* (also known as *chortens* which contain relics of the revered dead) at Bodinath, Swayambunath and the Hindu temple at Pashupatinath on the banks of the Baghmati. We were just in time to get a glimpse of Kumari the Living Goddess when she appeared on a balcony in Durbar Square. Traditionally the goddess is a young pre-pubescent girl who represents the divine female energy and is chosen from the silver smiths' caste of the Newari tribe.

I admired the pagodas and palaces of Kathmandu, Patan and Bhaktapur. All these old monuments are constructed with bricks and carved wood. The wood carving by the Newaris tribe of Nepal is one of the highest developed forms of craftsmanship in the world.

Hindu Shrine Kathmandu

Gods in the sky Kathmandu

Day 3.
MONDAY APRIL 4 1977
KATHMANDU/PHAPLU 8,000 feet

Yesterday we were introduced to a young Tibetan who lives in Darjeeling; his studies are sponsored by Gerard, a Brazilian (one of our group) who takes a general interest in his welfare. He was at the airport to wish us a safe journey and presented us with white Tibetan *kataks* (ceremonial scarves) as a farewell gesture because he was returning to Darjeeling. I was touched and impressed with his good manners and sincerity.

I was startled at the sight of our plane and thrilled to bits. Our aircraft was a Pilatus Porter. It was incredible that this tiny plane had the power to take us over the mountains on our way to Everest. This was so exciting that any lingering doubts I had about my health vanished in a flash as we flew above the top of the world over the Himalaya; below us lay an endless line of snow-capped mountains, - Everest, Annapurna, Himachuli, - far too many names to remember.

This was the land of legend and adventure previously only read about, and now I was part of it. I was finally on my way to Everest. You can keep your Jumbo jets and Airbuses, this is really flying. Soaring away above the clouds, I was breathless with excitement. Our pilot Captain Wick was on loan from Swiss Airlines to the Royal Nepal Airlines. He had achieved the most incredible exploits with this tiny machine including flights over Everest, once landing on a glacier.

Twenty minutes later after a hair raising flight through the mountains the plane banked to the right and dropped quickly down on to the airstrip at Phaplu, which was nothing more than a large field with a couple of huts perched on the side of a mountain, so dangerous there is no margin for error. Several men and woman with tiny children, all wearing the same dirty brown cotton garments watched us. I felt like visiting royalty as I descended from the plane.

Our first camp was already erected on the hillside and we were introduced to the Sherpas who would be our friends and porters for the next two weeks. The fires were lit and lunch was ready. I was ravenous and soon made short work of the chips, tomatoes, carrots and spam, followed by banana fritters. I looked enviously at the Sherpas who had huge piles of rice, lentil curry (*dhal*) and vegetables with chilli peppers which looked very tasty and I wondered if I could change my food to that of Sherpas.

The Sherpas are Buddhist people who live in the Everest region and are Tibetan in origin. They inhabit the Khumbu region in northeast Nepal and Darjeeling. They are one of Nepal's ethnic groups and one of 50 tribes who used to make their living trading with Tibet until China closed the border. Now they act as guides and porters.

We soon became used to our new routine; our homes were now tents. We would be woken up at the crack of dawn with 'bed' tea and a basin of water for washing, followed by breakfast. We were on the trail by seven o'clock with a brief stop for lunch, finally reaching our overnight destination by late afternoon. After supper we were all in our sleeping bags by eight and slept.

I soon found the trekkers' diet of cold meat and chips for main meals insubstantial and after checking with Chatuman the cook, I switched to the porters' food of *dhal baht* (rice, lentil curry) and fiery chilli peppers, very satisfying and I was full of energy.

Our Pilatus Porter aircraft with Valerie my tent mate

It was then I discovered, as the sun got hotter, my umbrella was missing and I must at all costs buy another. I would need it to keep the rain off, as a sunshade and a walking stick.

The afternoon was hot and we were all rather sleepy. I was contented to sit and admire the beautiful scenery - the tiny blue primulas at my feet dotted amongst the rocks which are flecked with mica. The glitter from the stones was dazzling.

My dream state did not last long; we were back on our feet again to set off on a trip to Salleri. Pam our British guide organized a Sherpa to go with us even though it was only half an hour down the hill; nothing was measured in miles here. I looked a glamourous sight in my walking boots, shorts, and caftan, to complete my ensemble a bush hat to keep off the sun. I was definitely the last word in chic!

At Salleri, I drew a blank, no umbrellas anywhere. However I was assured that I would definitely get one in the next village, a little further on. At this announcement, a few of the party decided to return to camp. There was no stopping me; I had to have an umbrella. I bought one eventually, a big black one, the kind we used to call a 'gamp,' with an unmistakable rainbow handle, quite different from anyone else's umbrella. Very superior!

My arms turned red on the way back to camp. By now I was thirsty so I gratefully accepted a large tin mug of black sweet tea and an arrowroot biscuit from one of the Sherpas.

We did not have much time for a rest as we had been invited to visit the small single storey hospital built by the Himalayan Trust and staffed by New Zealand doctors. The Himalayan Trust aims to improve the health, education and general wellbeing of the Sherpa people and is an international non-profit humanitarian organization first established in the 1960s by Sir Edmund

Hillary. It was his way of expressing his gratitude for the Sherpas' help when he was the first man together with Tenzing Norgay to conquer Everest in 1953.

In spite of the hospital's small size, I was impressed that it had all the basic ingredients including an x-ray machine and an operating theatre. The hot water was plentiful and completely free as it was solar heated. The patients were mainly Sherpas who brought their own bedding and food; paying only one rupee for the cost of their treatment. Their relatives stayed with them but slept in small huts which looked like bathing cubicles.

Pam and I went to the New Sherpa Hostelry, a short way up the hill. I thought the Hostelry had been built for Sherpas but it was also designed to cope with the ever-increasing flow of tourists coming to the Khumbu district who did not want to sleep in tents.

Our guide round this establishment was an important VIP gentleman whose name was Mr Bataraja or something similar. He held a high position in the government and had visited England and Italy in 1955. He became acquainted with the famous Himalayan writers and explorers Professor David Snellgrove and Giuseppe Tucci who had travelled widely throughout Nepal. How I wished that I had had the opportunity to meet such distinguished people. Mr Bataraja, a professor of African and Asian Studies now spends most of his time training suitable people as tourist guides.

The interior was richly and tastefully decorated. The main downstairs room was used for dining and seating. The walls of stained wood were covered in hand painted murals of Hindu and Buddhist images. The furniture mostly leather chairs and highly polished tables were luxurious. We saw the bedrooms and showers, all with cedar panelled walls and electric imitation oil lamps and I wondered that so much luxury had come to the mountains.

The hostelry would certainly encourage more tourists to come and change the face of Phaplu. Whether or not this is a good idea has caused a lot of controversy. However I think a little more money or help can only bring benefit to the Sherpa people. All foreigners bring change simply by being there and not always for the better. Alas this is progress and when we venture into unexplored regions, we should try to do our best not to influence the local culture by our habits and ideas. My homily for the day

Back to camp having done enough for today. It was early supper and bed by 7.30pm. At last we were surrounded by the great mountains with Numbur and Karyoling dominating the distant end of the valley.

Day 4.
TUESDAY APRIL 5
PHAPLU/RINGMO 9.000 feet (5.30 hours approx)

At 1am, I was wide awake; the bright full moon had completely fooled me. I thought it was morning just before sunrise and time to get up. My tent mate Valerie was horrified and shushed me into silence. Eventually I managed to get back to sleep until 5am when the Sherpas came to wake us up with 'bed' tea; very welcome as it was quite cool and we needed something hot to rouse us into some semblance of the stalwart trekkers we hoped to be.

From then on it was a mad rush, the porters descended on us to dismantle the tents and take our kitbags, those of us who had them. I was lucky I had mine. Breakfast at 6.30 was a feast of porridge, eggs and masses of toast and jam. I was so hungry I ate everything and those who still had stomachs after Kathmandu's culinary delights did likewise.

The morning's walk began through a pine forest in the beautiful Beni Khala valley, crossing little streams. We often stopped to admire the rhododendrons and primulas. I was stunned by the sight of a magnolia tree which had enormous star spangled white blooms hanging from the branches.

From time to time we would stop to eat sweets or offer cigarettes to the Sherpas and porters. The Sherpanis (the lady porters) preferred sweets and would receive them with shy giggles. They were very young to be carrying such heavy loads of up to 80 lbs (36 kilos), yet they did not show any strain and life certainly seem to suit them. A couple of the girls were beautiful with their rosy cheeks and pretty smiles.

Before we came to the village of Chiwang, we passed the first of many *mani* walls, made with stones engraved with Buddhist mantras or prayers. We were instructed that we should pass to the left hand side saying the Buddhist prayer, *'Om mani padme aum.'* (Hail to the jewel in the lotus.) Repeating this mantra gives merits towards the next life. Sometimes these walls were hard to spot but there was always a Sherpa to guide us gently in the right direction.

Lunch was early at 11am and we were ready for it. However we were not allowed to relax for long as the clouds were gathering and it started to rain. It remained showery for the rest of the afternoon.

We passed a tea house which was nothing more than a hut made from stones and we all rushed in, out of the rain to taste the legendary drink of *chang*, the local beer for the first time which was cross between cider and lager, it is made from fermented barley or millet. It looked like thick milk but was more like porridge in consistency. When I reached the bottom of the glass, I sifted the grits through my teeth. I liked it very much.

However I could see that I was in the minority and the only one keen to have another glass. At 1 rupee a glass I could certainly afford it. The other trekkers nodded and tasted politely but I could see I was going to be a loner on this journey. Already a gap was coming between me and the others.

We arrived at the camp site to find that the tents were up; tea was ready and the rest of the trekkers' kit plus stools and tables had arrived. This was camping in luxury and I felt that it was totally unnecessary to carry so much equipment. However I remained silent because there had been complaints last night about the discomfort of sitting on the ground. My comments would not help the situation.

The rain stopped so I walked a little way up the hill to the *mani* wall to get a better view of the mountain peaks covered in snow and ice which were emerging from the mist. They seemed to be only a mile or two away.

I was so exhilarated with the experience that I wanted to share some of my happiness with the others. I returned and dug out my Irish whiskey and handed it round. I was a little drunk by the time supper arrived. It certainly takes less whiskey to get inebriated at this altitude. Everyone else was as sober as judges and although I tried to inject a party atmosphere nobody was in a mood to join me. I only hoped that they would unbend later on.

At supper I ate the same food as the Sherpas, my plate piled high with rice and a meat mixture topped with fiery red chillis. I dodged the chillis but found the substantial meal satisfying. There was nothing to do after supper, so it was early to bed for a crack of dawn start next day.

Day 5.
WEDNESDAY APRIL 6 1977
RINGMO RIVER over TASKINDO PASS 12,696 feet to JUBING RIVER 5200 feet (6 hours approx)

I slept badly; I can't get used to these early bedtimes. As dusk falls it's a scramble to get to bed fast before night descends. When I finally woke up to my relief I had no hangover.

After breakfast, we raced behind the bushes as the toilet tents had been removed ahead of our stomachs. The sun was shining and it promised to be a hot day. We climbed steeply, puffing away, legs aching, up the Taksindo Pass. It was bliss when we got there.

On the way we passed several *mani* walls, chortens, stupas, and prayer flags. We dropped in on a *gompa* (monastery) but all we saw was a huge prayer wheel, the lama being away. Strangely I was the only one to be offered tea.

When I thought my legs would never move again, we came out of the gloom of the forest into the hot sunshine to an open cultivated terrace area with many fruit trees in bloom. We stopped for lunch at Muntale, a hamlet with four houses and found a small school built by Sir Edmund Hillary in thanks to the Sherpas for their help in mountain expeditions.

The children were dirty and delightful, ranging in age from about six to thirteen years old. We had been advised to bring small gifts with us and I felt like Santa Claus as I distributed balloons and pens to the pupils.

David, one of the youngest in the group was an instant hit with his Polaroid camera taking photos of the whole school in a traditional group. How different they were from our school photos but I suspect more treasured. It was placed in a position of honour on the school wall. We were given a guided tour of the building which consisted of two classrooms decorated with posters including one on family planning.

The weather was misty at this altitude; the chilly dampness clung to us and made us shiver after the heat of the valley. Picking up our bags we descended into the forest. The giant trees were covered in moss which was creeping over the plants and boulders, smothering everything in a thick green carpet.

What a relief to be descending even though I had to watch each step as the path had been washed away by last year's monsoons. Occasionally I had glimpses of the valley below and the mountains in between the trees.

I had hoped to see the Blood Pheasant which I had read about in Iain Graham's book *Blood Pheasant;* an account of his search on a trek to Everest for these rare birds which live at nine to fifteen thousand feet. I was disappointed because all I could hear was its cry of 'Kik kik kik.' Sometimes I would get brilliant flashes of other birds as they flew across our path but I did not know their names.

The afternoon proved to be extremely hot after lunch and again we were descending, skipping daintily over the boulders and scree brought down by the rains. Once the fog had lifted, the sun was scorching and we donned our shorts in an effort to keep ourselves cool.

The Dudh Khosi River beckoned us its ice blue water glinted in the sun as it rushed down in torrents all the way from the Khumbu glacier. We took numerous photos of the Hillary suspension bridge which swayed alarmingly in the wind.

A couple of the more stalwart trekkers decided to stop and wash but it looked a little too chilly for me and I thought I would see what the campsite had to offer first. Our site for tonight was on somebody's potato terraces. I was glad that I waited for my wash as I found a little stream and had my first good clean-up since Kathmandu. Tonight we camped at Jubing.

Children at Hillary School Muntale

Day 6.
THURSDAY APRIL 7 1977
JUBING RIVER/KHARTE 9200 feet (7 hours approx)

Last night was the first good night's sleep on the trek, waking up only once to find a dazzling moon. It was surprisingly warm.

We left just before 7am and climbed steadily upwards to the Jubing village set amongst the boulders on the terraces with stone walls and bamboo waving in the breeze under a blue sky. The houses were thatched and I was told they belonged to the Rai people who were renowned for their courage and bravery. They have won respect for their daring in the Nepalese Army. Also it is employment and a way of escaping rural poverty. They are one of Nepal's oldest ethno-linguistic groups living west of the Arun River in the area drained by Sun Khosi River. They also live in S.W. Bhutan and Sikkim.

I found that I was climbing a little too fast and I was soon out of breath. One has to take things a little easier the higher we climb. At one time, I dragged behind the others and got lost. I called out and fortunately Pemba our Sirdar (Head Sherpa) saw me. Hastily I scrambled down through the barley terraces back on the right path. We could afford to go a little steadier now as the path was flat, ridge way walking, easy in the heat after all that climbing.

Finally we reached Karikhola which was a delightful Sherpa village with two-story houses of hand-cut stone, many windows with a coloured frame. Sometimes there was a patio with a prayer pole and a fluttering prayer flag. The vegetable gardens were strewn with marigolds, roses, cosmos and banana trees. Incredible! Imagine finding bananas growing at 9,000 feet.

Here we made another 'Royal Visit' to the local school. One of our Sherpas,

Thondup had struck up a conversation with one of the local ladies who he claimed was his wife. A moment later she hurried away to return with a large jug of *raksi* (wine spirit tasting like Irish poteen made from rice or millet). Pemba and Thondup made me take more than my share. Have you ever poured surgical spirit down your throat? That's what it felt like. From now on I would stick to *chang*.

The lunch stop was a pretty place and I happily tucked into a dish of *chura* (Sherpa dish of rice moistened with tea topped with chillis and onions) both tasty and satisfying. We were climbing again after lunch which made me breathless. I had a rest while the others went to the *chang* house.

When we had reached 10,000 feet, members of the group confessed they were beginning to disintegrate. From the start of the trek Doris our married lady hated every minute and wants to go home. She was also feeling ill. The absence of all her familiar surroundings, no doctors, telephones or roads were making her feel insecure. Tomorrow she will fly back to Kathmandu from Lukla. David since his gastric attack in Kathmandu has been living on antibiotics and will stay on them for the rest of the trek. Fortunately he was feeling a little better. I was surprised the way he has kept going without complaint. Most of the others have suffered either bowel or stomach upsets or both. I was sure that eating the local food which is spicy and therefore antiseptic has saved me from catching any bugs.

Tonight's campsite was waterless which has saved us the bother of washing, our quickie wipes will come in handy and we can wash our teeth in tea. Our surroundings were magical as we were situated in a forest clearing, circled by huge magnolia trees in bloom. Nobody cared about the washing water.

There was a rush to get the tents up before the storm broke and we got inside just in time. There was a deafening clap of thunder followed by lightning, rain and hailstones the size of peas which descended all at the same time. When I stuck my head out of the tent all I could see were hailstones an inch thick on the ground, the place was completely white.

Kristi the youngest woman in the party and I had decided to do our exercises that evening, a set of Surya Namaskars or Sun Prayers based on Yoga positions but we had to cancel them. Rain had stopped play.

Day 7.
FRIDAY APRIL 8 1977
KHARTE over KHARTE PASS/CHANDRIKARKA 10,300 feet (7 hours approx)

Heavens, it was cold last night! Just on freezing point. At what seemed like the crack of dawn I found it hard to get out of my cozy sleeping bag and when a steaming hot mug of bed tea arrived it was extremely welcome. There was no time to linger; breakfast was ready before we were. Fortunately we saved a little time by not washing. No water does have its advantages.

Strolling through the forests I found many of the shrubs we have in England, several tree orchids and two types of primulas I had not seen before. This was a botanist and a bird-watcher paradise. There were supposed to be some monkeys but I never saw one.

As we came out of the forest and climbed the Kharte Pass (10,300 feet) a spectacular panorama of mountain peaks was spread before us. This is yak country so Dolly and I had our picture taken with one of them for posterity. Situated at the top of the pass was a most welcome tea house where we revived ourselves with cups of hot sweet tea. Then we were back on our feet again until we stopped for lunch by the Dudh Khosi River. After a short rest we descended into the forest and from the top of the next pass as we looked down to the right we could see Lukla air-strip and to the left the village of Chaunrikharka.

Me Dolly and the yak

We met many people on the path, mostly Tamangs travelling to and from Namche Bazaar markets who responded to our greetings. They are the largest

Tibeto-Burman ethnic group within Nepal and are Buddhist. They originally came from Tibet and were given the name Tamang because they were horse traders. 'Ta' in Tibetan means horse man or trader.

A few trekkers sometimes passed us in groups but mostly in pairs. Today we met some Tibetan lamas who had stopped by the wayside but when we enquired if we could take their photos, they refused and regarded our cameras with suspicion. We made up for our cheek by compensating them with some sweets which were accepted.

Kristi and I travelled with the Sherpa Thondup this afternoon and what fun we had. We laughed all the way. Out of sight of the others, Thondup kept going into the chang houses and although normally he was rather reserved, the more he drank the more garrulous he became. Despite his lack of English we managed to make ourselves understood. We were delighted when he brought us garlands of rhododendrons.

Tonight we were supposed to have camped at Surke a small village built just above the spot where the Dudh Kosi joins the Umding Khola but there were no fields to spare for the tents. We had no option but to press on to the next village – Chaunrikharka - where many of the Sherpas have their homes.

Poor Doris was suffering and has dragged behind even with help from Nima the Sherpa. She was depressed with the trek hating every step and was rather scared of being so far away from civilization. Plans have been made for her to fly back to Kathmandu, probably tomorrow from Lukla which is close by.

The rain started to fall in big drops; hastily we tied our cagoules round our shoulders and up went our brollies. Ever forward, up and down, staggering and slipping in the mud we finally reached the comfort of Chaunrikharka in the pouring rain.

The porters were exhausted, the loads were damp and everyone seemed dejected. Tea would be wonderful but it was going to be a long time in coming. Passing the houses someone called out our names, we looked up and in the gathering gloom we could see some of our party in a Sherpa house which belonged to Pemba the Sirdar. We made our way through the downstairs room used as a stable and climbed up the staircase to the main room.

The room was dark and full of trekkers and Sherpas. Mrs Pemba bustled round pressing welcome cups of tea into our hands. It was absolute bliss to sit cross-legged on the mats in the warm room. I watched the firelight flickering on the copperware on the dresser, lighting up the faces which in an instant was gone when the door opened and a sudden draught of air blew the smoke everywhere. The Sherpas have no chimneys to their houses so the smoke filters through the roof.

After tea was drunk, the chang arrived, cup after cup of the brew and we were urged to, 'Che che' which meant 'Drink drink,' I needed no second invitation, after all the walking for the day. How delicious it was, I soon felt warm and cozy and a little bit high and in love with the Sherpas who are so kind to strangers.

Finally I reluctantly got to my feet and walked with the others to the camp site to find the tents were up and soaking wet. Our leak ran straight down the middle of the tent from back to front. In that downpour it was inadvisable to unpack this turned out to be a fortunate decision because after supper disaster had struck and the tent was flooded. Fortunately our kit was just out of reach of the water and dry so we evacuated immediately.

Pemba decided we would sleep at his house. My tent mate Valerie and I packed a few necessities for the night and accompanied by Pam our leader set off for the night to our new billet. I was thrilled and blessed the rain gods for flooding us out.

Pemba Mrs Pemba baby girl

More glasses of chang were called for, 'Ah this was the life!' The children were a little shy but soon became used to us when we tried to make friends with them. We chatted for some time by the fire looking at photos proudly shown to us by Pemba's father, of his son.

The chang had taken its toll, I was desperate for a bathroom and I had no idea where it was. Fortunately Pam soon found it and took us to a little house standing apart from the others which was a communal lavatory. Spotlessly clean, it was little more than a hole in the floor where everything fell into dry leaves below. In spring the loos are emptied and the rotted manure is spread on the fields. There was no smell due to the altitude. Nothing here is wasted.

Our bedroom was the small family temple leading from the main room. We were give mats in front of the altar and slept like a log under Buddha's benevolent gaze. We must have walked twenty miles today. The fire died down and Pemba, his wife and baby girl retired to their bed in the living room and all was quiet.

Day 8.
SATURDAY APRIL 9 1977
CHANDRIKARKA/JORSALE   9,000 feet (approx 6 hours)

We were woken by the old man who shared our room saying his prayers so I said a couple too. Pemba made us some butter salted Sherpa tea which I find I am getting a taste for.

Arriving back at camp, everyone was in an uproar. Many had had a damp night and Gerard was annoyed his lilo had sprung a leak and he was forced to lie on the hard ground. It was a mad scramble to our kitbags (fortunately they had escaped a wetting) while the tents were being pulled down round us. The call of 'Breakfast,' made me jump and I nearly dropped my contact lenses in the porridge when it arrived.

The sun was watery and rain was promised. Ignoring the ominous weather signs we decided to go back to Pemba's house to take some photos of the family and also I wanted to give Mrs Pemba a small present for her kindness. Not much fun for her to have strangers in her home when she had not seen her husband for several weeks. My gift selection was limited so I settled on some socks for Mrs P. and some sweets for the child. I would have liked to have stayed in Chaunrikharka and explored the village but alas we had to move on. Doris left this morning for Lukla and was put on a flight to Kathmandu.

The morning walk was easy at last there was some respite after yesterday's marathon. We passed through undulating country dotted profusely with *mani* walls and *chortens*. Some of the *mani* walls were just boulders intricately carved with prayers. Others were walls of stones carved in the same manner. I wondered at the patience of the artisans who had produced these works of art. Many of the stones were very old. One was erected in memory of a Sherpa who had died.

We crossed many bridges inspired and built by Edmund Hillary. As we wandered through the forest admiring the rhododendrons, we caught glimpses of the snow clad Thamserku between the pine and oak trees. The mountains kept appearing from time to time like bit-part actors.

Lunch was by the Dudh Kosi River at Phakding and we sweltered in the heat. I found a small private place on a rock along the river bank to have a good wash. Afterwards I found a small shop which sold a limited range of goods and I bought some biscuits and ½ kilo of boiled sweets. My supply of chocolate and sweets was running low and although I used to distribute my chocolate after a while I became cunning and ate it secretly. I wasn't the only one who did this as chocolate was fast becoming a luxury item and it was considered a great honour to be offered a piece by one of the trekkers.

By common consent, lunch times were usually spent washing or catching up with our diaries. Often there is so much to record and too little time to write down all the details.

Today everyone has cheered up and there was less talk of bowels and stomachs. The depression from yesterday has lifted temporarily. I thought it was incredible that they were so preoccupied with themselves and their discomforts. I do not know why most of them have come on this trek and I think they are wondering about that as well. Perhaps it was simply the prestige of trekking to Everest. I am so engrossed in the journey that I keep forgetting about Everest. The journey has now become a way of life for me and is no longer a holiday.

Time to move on. once more we shouldered our packs and trailed along the river bank. Life was a little easier now. I was in my stride with this walk, I could go on forever. As the weather has turned a little cool, I reached for my favourite dirty grey sweater and then remembered I had left it behind a rock a few miles back at the lunch stop.

There was nothing for it but to return, I simply could not leave it behind so Thondup the Sherpa came back all the way with me. All the rocks looked alike and I had to start again from the beginning before I finally found the place where I had left it. I was amazed to see the sweater still there. I was so happy that I gave Thondup a bonus of two packs of cigarettes. The others would be mental that I upped the tipping rates if they found out. Still I was hardly likely to tell them. I don't understand why I am not gelling with this party; I normally get on well with people. I liked Dolly the best she was made redundant from her job in Southampton and originally from the east end of London and was good fun to be with.

To celebrate the reunion with my sweater Thondup and I stopped at every *chang* house on the way back to camp at the small village of Jorsale. We would have been very late but we found a quick route and arrived only just behind the others who had taken the scenic route. Thondup and I got on really well despite the language barrier.

In our absence Pemba had not been idle, after seeing Doris off on her plane to Kathmandu from Lukla; he had found some new tents for us. They were of a German make and infinitely superior to the others, we now had room to move about which was an advantage as tempers had got a little frayed when unfortunately I would wake my tent mate by accident when I wanted to go to the loo during the night.

Entertainment was laid on tonight after supper in the form of a camp fire. We sang songs and drank our booze. Alas that was the end of the Irish whiskey as I shared it with the Sherpas. I don't think they were too impressed but they were polite about it. I was flattered when Pemba pleased with my taste for Sherpa food and drink suggested,
'Come we go *chang* house more drinking.'

The others declined but after the heady freedom of the night before I agreed to go. The group were not too pleased at the idea of me going but graciously gave permission. Anyway I was full of the joys of spring and could have stayed up all night. At this stage I had imbibed so much alcohol that if anyone suggested we climbed Everest I would have agreed to it.

Accompanied by Pemba and Lakpa, I sallied forth. The *chang* house ladies had settled for the night but at the prospect of some business they soon revived the fire and reheated the *chang* in a huge kettle. After several glasses of *chang,* the whiskey and the altitude put us in a party mood, laughing and talking a lot. We were all drunk.

The night was dark, it was too early for the moon to rise and the return path was dangerous and slippery. Pemba led the way and cautiously we made our way back single file. Suddenly one of us slipped, I cannot remember to this day whether it was either Pemba or I but suddenly I found myself rolling over and over as I fell down the side of the mountain until a bush stopped my headlong progress downwards. Pemba had fallen with me but Lakpa was safe.

I went, until a bush stopped my headlong progress downwards. Pemba was unhurt but my back and face were badly strained and grazed. I was hurt, cold and frightened and did not want to move until daylight came. Maybe if I rested some of the pain would go from my back. Slowly but painfully I made my way back to camp. As I crawled into my tent I thought that I would never get on my feet again and that this was the end of my dream and I would be sent back to Kathmandu in disgrace. I made a vow that I would never mix *chang and* Irish whiskey again.

Day 9.
SUNDAY APRIL 10 1977
JORSALE /NAMCHE BAZAAR 9,200 feet (3 hours approx)

I had great difficulty getting up next morning; I spent most of the night in a fitful sleep. Every time I moved I woke up and the pain was terrible. My face, leg and back were bruised and grazed.

Fortunately I had not broken any bones and had just a few pulled muscles.

I had to explain my situation to the others, who were appalled so I gave them a watered-down version of the accident. I sensed hostility from some, understandably I suppose. I could have put the whole party in jeopardy with my behaviour. I knew it was not my fault but there was no point in saying anything in my defence because it would only have caused more trouble. I was determined this morning despite the pain to get myself to the end of the trek but first things first; I had to get to Namche Bazaar.

Luckily today we had only a half-day's trek ahead of us and I would be able to rest this afternoon. After a handful of aspirins I felt a bit better and slowly with the help of one of the porters, I completed the four-hour climb to Namche Bazaar. We climbed steadily through yesterday's gorge with the cliffs up to the sky gaining in altitude as we went. No-one was more surprised than me to reach the police post at Namche where I had a well earned rest.

After the fall down the mountain

The campsite was the worst I had seen so far; with rubbish strewn everywhere and parts of it had been used as a toilet. I am ashamed to say, by foreigners, as some of the litter was toilet paper.

Collapsing into my tent, I noticed that I had burst a blood vessel in one eye so I abandoned my contact lenses as one eye is too swollen. I looked as if I have been mugged. I confessed the extent of my injuries to the tour leader who told me to stay in bed. The group went into a huddle and decided I should go to the local hospital, five miles away.

Namche Bazaar

'Not likely,' I said. 'The walk would kill me! With a few aspirins I'll make it.'

After lunch, Pam dressed my back and I went back to bed, the others went into 'town' to see the sights. Traditionally the village is a trading post and the commercial area of the Solu Khumbu with the local Sherpa people bartering yak cheese and butter for agricultural goods grown at lower altitudes. However, after Sir Edmund Hillary and Tenzing Norgay's successful climb of Everest in 1953, the ways of the village have changed forever as climbers and trekkers soon followed in their wake. Although Namche now thrives through tourism it remains a small settlement with no more than about 60 dwellings.

Some of the group went to the town and the others went to the Hotel Everest View built in the 1960s by the Japanese and situated only a short distance away from the town and officially the highest hotel in the world at 12780 feet. The only access for tourists is by helicopter or the three day trek from Lukla.

Many Sherpas helped with the construction. Materials such as the sliding glass doors used in the rooms, the glass for the solarium, blankets and eating utensils imported from Japan. These were shipped to Calcutta and then transported to Nepal either by helicopter or by porters or yaks, as most of the journey was overland. Finally the hotel opened in 1971 to tourists who had limited time and lots of money who wanted to experience Everest. Flying in by helicopter from 5,000 to 9,000 feet does have its drawbacks, so oxygen tanks were made available for anyone suffering from altitude sickness.

I slept for a couple of hours and woke up feeling much brighter. On their return the others came to regale me with the good time they had eating pancakes in the town or meat burgers (they didn't know what kind), in the Hotel Everest View. They have all returned in a good mood after hitting the fleshpots of Namche. I was so happy when they came one by one to tell me of their adventures. I had expected to be ostracized and I would not have blamed them. I think they were being very decent about my escapade which turned out to be such absolute folly.

Hotel Everest View Solukhumbu

Day 10.
MONDAY APRIL 11 1977
NAMCHE BAZAAR /TENGBOCHE
12,715 feet (5 ½ hours approx)

Last night we had our first flurry of snow, and after a good sleep aided by a sleeping pill, I felt much better. The preliminary stiffness soon wore off and although it was rather agonizing getting up and down to a sitting position, for the first time I felt I was going to survive.

This morning was easy as we continued our journey along a level track following the Imja Khola which rushed along beside us. We found many small mountain iris and other small plants which I have not seen before. Across this tree-less valley, we were constantly aware of the ice bound mass of Thamserku which changed moods as the cloud passed over its surface. Finally we saw Everest, Lhotse, and Ama Dablam in all their full glory. I felt so emotional; the sight of such splendour moved me to tears. At last I had come all this way and there they were majestic in their snow covered grandeur against an azure sky.

Faraway in the distance, we glimpsed our destination - the monastery Tengboche - as we descended once more into the forest of moss-covered trees and rhododendrons. We crossed the Phungutenma Bridge across the Imja Khola to our lunch stop and found many prayer wheels powered by water in the village.

After lunch it was back on the 'up'. As we climbed we left our mossy glades and approached Tengboche, passing through a painted archway leading to the monastery. Tengboche is one of the most famous monasteries in Nepal, probably because Ama Dablam stands just behind it. The building was built in 1923 and destroyed by an earthquake in 1934 and rebuilt again. Tengboche Gompa, the biggest Buddhist monastery in Nepal, is also known as Dawa Choling Gompa. The famous Mani Rimdu Festival is celebrated here every year. Once it was famous for its learning in the days before the Chinese occupation of Tibet; monks and lamas from as far away as Lhasa made pilgrimages to this sacred place. Now the monastery has declined. Very few boys want to become monks, preferring to go to the towns to earn a more lucrative living there or becoming porters or guides to the many groups who pass this way.

Once the tents were up I set out to explore and found the local *chang* house full of trekkers and a Thomas Cook trekking group. I met a girl, Barbara travelling on her own. She had been with a party of Americans and New Zealanders but they had left her. She was too ill with the altitude and heat and I suspect overdosed on hash to continue her journey. I gave her my bush hat and left her to sleep.

We wrapped up in our warmest clothes for the camp fire after supper. We had been warned that this was going to be a cold camp. We had been invited by some German trekkers, who arrived looking like Michelin men in their duvet jackets and trousers, to join them after supper for a get-together. They were friendly but they were a hard crowd to talk to and rather starchy. This was probably due to the language barrier. Fortunately the Sherpas saved the day with their great pot of chang and their songs. I will never forget 'The Khukri Rum Song,' the song has haunted me ever since. They have the art of giving a good impromptu party.

Day 11.
TUESDAY APRIL 12 1977
TENGBOCHE (Day of rest)

My first thought when I woke up was 'Hurrah, my back is better.' We had our first snow last night, about six inches had

Tengboche Monastery.

fallen. How exciting! The sun was rising and was incredibly beautiful as the mountains came into full view and slowly came to life. I sat in silence huddled in my sleeping bag on a chair watching dawn break; breathless with excitement.

Today I have decided to rest, acclimatize to the altitude and enjoy the spectacular panorama in all directions of the famous mountains Nuptse and Lhotse with the plumed peak of Everest looking rather insignificant in between. (Everest is only 15 miles away as the crow flies from here.)

The glacier masses of the beautiful Thamserku , Kantega (within 10 miles), Taweche, Cholatse and Kumbila are overshadowed by the mysterious Ama Dablam, the sacred mountain whom nobody has ever been given permission to climb. Ama Dablam means 'Mother's necklace,' Ama meaning mother and Dablam the traditional pendant containing pictures of the gods worn by Sherpa women.

At breakfast, Pam produced a present for each of us, Easter chocolate bunnies, which was a lovely surprise. The Sherpas could not make head or tail of the custom when she tried to explain Easter to them.

Dhal baht lentil curry

We were privileged this morning, to be allowed to see the monastery. The walls were lined with ancient books, tankhas hung from the pillars and many Buddha statues stood in contemplation. A deep silence pervaded the atmosphere, occasionally broken by prayers intoned by a *lama* or the flash of a tourist's camera. The monk who showed us round collected a small donation from each of us. Wanting to be on my own for a moment or two, I stepped outside for some peace and quiet and waited for the others.

Pam came looking for me with a present; a Tibetan prayer flag, black and white on fragile parchment-like-paper. The flags were luck-commanding talismans. Ours were 'victorious banner' flags which contained several spells to Durga the consort of Shiva and brought not only luck in life and wealth but also increased the powers of the individual. We were all given one. I was feeling a little guilty because the others had given presents of a Parker pen and sweets and I had only donated a few rupees.

The snow disappeared and we spent the rest of the day sunbathing. At last Kristi and I managed a few of our special exercises, the Surya Namaskars or Sun Prayers.

The afternoon was spent as usual in the *chang house* chatting to the passing tourists mostly American and some British. There was no one interesting to talk to; I could have done with one of the paper backs I left in Kathmandu. Even my knitting would have passed the time happily. Rather bored.

Resting their loads at Tengboche

Yet another camp fire tonight and I gave Pemba fifty rupees for *chang* for the staff. I had invited David an American teacher who I met in the *chang* house to come to our party. He had just come from Taiwan and had been travelling solo all over Asia for some time. He had a degree in philosophy. I found him interesting and it was nice to have someone to talk to for a change. I was amazed when the Sherpas developed a hostile attitude towards him, I thought he was quite harmless and also my guest

I heard later that some of these lone travellers are rogues and tend to cheat the people. It is common practice to order food and a night's lodging to be paid for in the morning but leave without paying, in an area short of food and money, the local people were becoming cautious. Their good nature and hospitality imposed on too often.

I finally got to bed at 11.00 pm having consumed prodigious amounts of *chang*. I have developed a taste for the drink and am rapidly becoming a *chang*-alcoholic. I simply must learn how to make it.

Glass of chang

Day 12.
WEDNESDAY APRIL 13 1977
TENGBOCHE/DINGBOCHE   14,400 feet (6 hours approx)

I decided today to carry my own day pack and do without my 'modern convenience,' my Sherpa. During the lunch break I found a good clean stream and had my first good wash for days, water was non-existent at Tengboche. I hung the wet clothes on my rucksack to dry. Lapka who was following a little way behind had the tedious task of explaining to Nepali passersby who asked what had happened to my face now a mass of healing grazes and looking far worse than it was.

The scenery changed dramatically in the afternoon, the higher we went the more desolate it became. We were in a wilderness where there was nothing except stones and dust, all a different shade of grey. The only vegetation was a few thorn bushes and stunted juniper bushes. We had reached the glacial valleys above the tree line where the nomads bring their yaks to graze in summer.

I was walking very slowly so I did not feel the altitude. Although I longed to sit down for a rest I was afraid that I would never get up again if I succumbed to the temptation. To my surprise I found that my eyesight is perfect up here without my contact lenses and the only real discomfort I was feeling was the weight of my rucksack which was glued to my back.

I have spent today on my own; I am tired of my companions and their problems. The cold wind blew incessantly; it was the only companion I needed.

Our resting place was in the middle of nowhere, just desolation and not a *chang* house in sight for the weary traveller. I love these places not just for the chang but the gossip from a wide variety of trekkers of all nationalities. The only habitation was a couple of yak huts which Chatuman our cook used as a kitchen. Looking at the terrain I can hardly believe that yaks come up here in summer. There is not a blade of grass in sight.

Day 13.
THURSDAY APRIL 14 1977
DINGBOCHE (Day of rest)

Today was an altitude acclimatization day and a day of rest for the big push forward with absolutely nothing to do and nowhere to go. Hm! No books, knitting, games, so I will have to use my ingenuity instead to fill the day. What a dump!

I went up to the local pipeline and did the washing. That was okay. Encouraged by my achievement I decided to wash my hair. What a disaster, the water was freezing and my hair threatened to turn into icicles and fall out at the roots.

I searched around for something else to do and looked at the rubbish. Maybe I could tidy that up a bit. I abandoned the idea as fast as it had come. Where to put it posed another problem with no dustbin collections up here. The ground was too frozen to dig so I could not bury it. If I really get too bored I suppose I could always read the labels.

Two of Kristi's friends, doctors in the small hospital at Pheriche, arrived in the middle of the morning. I was horrified that no one thought to offer them any refreshment. Delighted at the prospect of visitors and something to do, I unearthed my secret store of precious Nescafe and Compliment dried milk and persuaded Chatuman to boil some water so I was able to serve coffee to anyone who wanted it.

It was then I noticed my sunburned arms were badly blistered by the wind. Fortunately I had dressings, large enough to cover them. I am looking very odd, with my grazed face; white cuffs on my burnt arms and of course my rotten back. I have declared myself a National Disaster Area.

I spent the rest of the morning in the kitchen eating potatoes, chilli powder and salt; chatting to Pemba and Chatuman who used to be a soldier in the Gurkha regiment but was now a cook for tourist groups.

Lunch was exceptional today, more potatoes, home-made chutney (tomatoes, garlic, onions, chilli, salt and turmeric.) I ate so much I could hardly move. I am the only one putting on weight, everyone else was visibly fading otherwise we all look well with our suntans despite the sores on our faces and fingers.

To shake down the food, a few of us went for a walk but we did not go too far, the overcast sky chased us back to our tents when the snow started to fall.

Ailsa is suffering badly from altitude sickness with a severe headache and swollen limbs. Pam has given her a lasex tablet for the fluid retention but it does not seemed to have helped. She will have to go down tomorrow to Pheriche Hospital accompanied by Thondup.

Day 14.
FRIDAY APRIL 15 1977
DINGBOCHE/LOBUJE 16,175 feet (5 hours approx)

The thunderstorm which rattled non-stop during the night plus a dog's constant howling and three inches of snow, guaranteed that the group would be in a bad mood this morning. The cold nibbled at our fingers and noses as we hurried to pack our kitbags and ate our breakfast quickly. An extra helping of porridge was most welcome.

My back has improved with the rest and I have managed to cut down my daily fix of aspirins by half. For a change I led the way with the advance porters; the snow swept scene was straight out of James Hilton's *'Lost Horizon.'* This was our first walk through the snow and hard going, snowflakes obliterating the path in many places.

Slowly we plodded steadily up the wind-swept valley. We were now above the tree line and all around us were desert moraine vegetation, boulders, frozen water-falls and absolute desolation. Just below the pass we caught sight of Lobuje where we will camp for the night.

Pleased to be the first at the lunch stop at Thaklu, I headed for the *chang* house to have tea, a little too early in the day for *chang*. My scruples were soon overcome and I treated myself to one, it was far too cold to wait outside for lunch. Today was the coldest day so far. Lunch was a long time coming as Chatuman was working under appalling conditions. I chose *chura* and gulping it down as fast as possible, I obtained Pam's permission and set off through the blizzard after the

Thomas Cook group. I did not want to hang about any longer.

At the top of the ridge were eight stupas commemorating the death of eight Sherpas who were killed in an avalanche. Known as a place of ill-omen, all who those passed this way quickened their pace. The snow fell heavily all afternoon and I missed the promised views of Ama Dablam because I was too intent on keeping to the path.

Lobuje was another of those desolate campsites but this was at least livened up by two 'hotels' or rather glorified tea houses. Gerard and I made straight for the first one and found seats by the smoky fire, prepared to wait until the porters arrived with the kit. The proprietor tried to charge us two rupees a glass for chang but after a bit of bargaining we got it down to the correct price. I found out later that our behaviour was wrong as the higher you go the dearer everything becomes and it is wrong for foreigners to bargain in these places. It just makes them look ignorant which we were because no-one had told us not to bargain over food and drink.

This 'hotel' was better than others we had seen with seats round the fire, the ones by the wall being used for beds at night. It was roughly built from loose stones, roofed with corrugated sheeting held down by stones. The smoke from the juniper wood got in our eyes and made me cough, however it was sheer bliss to be out of the wind so no-one complained.

The wind was blowing fiercely and the prospect of sitting in a cold tent was not inviting. Might have been better if I had had some whiskey, but alas that was all gone and there was nothing for it but to put on some more clothes and return to the fire.

A Yugoslav diplomat and his wife, both in their fifties had arrived and were settling in for the night. They had come from Burma and had covered the trek from Phaphlu to Lobuje in a short time. I admired their stamina travelling the hard way with only one porter and staying in the tea houses. I noticed they carried their own food which was a wise precaution. Their meal tonight was chicken noodle soup.

***Chura* a Sherpa dish of rice moistened with tea**

Tonight we were camping high above the tree line in the desolation of snow and ice on the Khumbu glacier.

There would be absolutely no washing this evening.

Day 15.
SATURDAY APRIL 16 1977
LOBUJE (Day of rest)

We have had the most peculiar places for rest days. The best one so far was Tengboche. They were programmed to give us the maximum time to adjust to the higher altitudes on just the right days. Several of the party were now feeling very tired.

Valerie's Max and Min thermometer recorded that last night was the coldest registering -15 degrees C. We thought it must be wrong but we had forgotten that the Khumbu glacier was not exactly a hot spot. My water bottle and cider vinegar, the latter used for keeping a bug-free stomach were both frozen solid. Instead we improvised and brushed our teeth in tea.

What a miserable bunch of trekkers we were at breakfast even Terry, the architect who always looked dapper looked a little frail. Everyone was wishing they had not come and they would go back tomorrow if they could. Thank goodness when the hot food arrived everybody cheered up.

The Khumbu Glacier

There was some talk of Gerard, myself and a couple of the others leaving for base camp Everest (this was the South base camp) for the night but this was whittled down to Gerard and myself. The others were not fit enough so the project was cancelled as the Sherpas could not be spared and it would also mean cold food for 24 hours, a fate worse than death in this temperature.

We made do with a leisurely stroll up and down the hills near the camp. The views of Lhotse and Pumari were magnificent. There were so many mountains again I could not keep pace with the names.

When the wind dropped and the sun was shining, a couple of the women tried to improve their tans in the heat. Gerrard, every time the sun appeared, would disrobe donning a small pair of bathing shorts which would have been more suitable for a beach in the south of France. The man never ceased to amaze me; he managed to keep up appearances at all times. I wondered when he would give up shaving but he never did.

Camping at Lobuje

I took Dolly to the 'hotel' to meet the Yugoslavians and they gave us some chocolate. Definitely the highlight of the day and we were the envy of our fellow trekkers.

The group went to bed after lunch; I was not tired so I went for a walk finding a little hollow in the rocks sheltered from the wind and the occasional snow shower. I dozed while I watched the birds which looked like sand martins played round my feet. They were very tame and not at all afraid of me. I was getting a little too cozy, time to move so I got on my feet and galloped off to the 'hotel' to see if there was any fresh gossip and a glass of *chang*.

The place was dead. I was welcomed as a regular by the owner, a glass of *chang* was placed in my hand and some more juniper wood was put on the fire. I sat back lazily and watched the snow fall slowly outside. This was heaven! I was far more at home here than I would have been in an English pub.

Two Tibetans, one belonging to our group and the other to the Thomas Cooke party had been doing a little business on the side concerning their yaks. Money changed hands and some sacks of potatoes were left by the door. The money safe was an old battered tin. I could not understand a word; all I could do was to sit back happily with my *chang* wondering what news they were discussing.

Things started to liven up. A young American couple Marilyn and Ed came in all resplendent in blue duvet jackets looking very clean and healthy. They were trekking on their own having been badly let down by one of the travel companies and were able to give me news from Gorakshep and Tengboche. Barbara the sick girl I met at Tengboche had given up and was heading back to Calcutta.

There had been the devil of a row at Gorakshep which nearly turned to violence when one of the Americans travelling on their own had lost a camera and had refused to tip the Sherpa who found it. It was a nasty incident. The American had accused the Sherpa of stealing it. Gorakshep was not the place to cause a fight, in these mountains it was easy to disappear without trace if you were on your own.

One by one the Sherpas came into the warmth of the fire. I felt filthy rich when I ordered drinks all round, at a cost of 30 pence! I like *chang* a lot better than beer and could sit happily in an alcoholic haze, contented to be here.

At this altitude we were always ravenous except for those with 'stomachs and bowels' and tonight's supper was full of surprises. First of all there was soup followed by *tupka* (noodles with meat soup) and lastly the Chef's Special, a cake made by the fourteen year old boy assistant in a pressure cooker! We loved it and ate the lot. To wash it down we drank sweet milk-less tea drowned in Kukri rum. Wow! After that lot we could not move.

Tupka Noodles in Meat Soup

Day 16.
SUNDAY APRIL 17 1977
LOBUJE/GORAKSHEP-KALAPATAR
18,175 feet (3 hours approx)

Reveille was at 4am and we were up and off to Gorakshep. This was our final stage and our plan was to climb Kalapatar, another 1000 feet higher than Gorakshep and the equivalent of second camp on Everest. From the summit we hoped to see the panoramic view of all the mountains which surrounded us.

With my breakfast unfinished, a piece of bread in one hand and my rucksack in the other we set off at 4.30am in the pitch dark. There were a few casualties this morning. I really admired the way the sick ones were determined to make it to the bitter end when most of them should have been tucked up in bed with a hot water bottle.

I was feeling really fit, my back was better and my breathing was OK as long as I went slowly. Young David and I were determined to get to the summit. David to take his photographs and me, I just wanted to get to the 'end.'

The snow was falling lightly as we left wearing our warmest clothes and I was grateful to Valerie for lending me an extra pair of mittens. We clambered over the boulders and rubble of the Khumbu Glacier, some of it easy some of it hard.

The place was dead, no vegetation, no people not even a sign of a house, all we had for company was snow, and the wind which blew constantly.

A blizzard was blowing when we stumbled into the 'hotel' at Gorakshep which was crammed to suffocation with Americans, the Thomas Cooke group and a few odd trekkers. Some of them appeared to be suffering from altitude and there was a general air of unease amongst solitary trekkers. It was most definitely not the place to linger.

There was some talk as to whether it was wise to climb Kalapatar in this bad weather. Pemba thought it would be alright and detailed Nima to come with the five of us who had elected to go the last 1000 feet, even though we would probably see nothing from the top. David, Norman, Kristi, Dolly and I were considered completely mad by the others so they said they would wait for us.

There was no recognizable path and it was hard going up zigzagging all the way. Dolly had enough at 600 feet, planted her little Union Jack which she had brought from the UK and went back down to Gorakshep. We were within thirty yards of the summit when I felt I could go no further but the others encouraged me to keep going. I found it so difficult jumping from boulder to boulder, scrambling over scree, everything blotted out by snow.

At this altitude (18,175 feet) we hoped to see the glorious panorama of mountains from the top. Alas, we didn't. The snow refused to stop. We celebrated at the top with some of David's chocolate kept especially for the occasion and some cheese which Pemba had brought up for us, racing up the mountain like a goat, his agility putting us to shame.

My boots were bad for this type of walking and to make things worse they were now soaking wet. On the return journey I lagged behind. The snow obliterated the path as it fell. Slipping and sliding at every step, I slowly made the long journey back to the comfort of the tea house at Gorakshep. When I arrived I wept all over Dolly who was still there, I gratefully devoured some chapattis and jam brought up from the camp by Chatuman.

Kalapatar 18,175 feet

Gerard had elected to stay the night so Lapka returned to camp to fetch his sleeping bag and lilo to give him a little comfort for the night, if he could find space to lie down. He hoped the weather might be better tomorrow morning. He would have to complete two days trekking in one to catch up with the group. At fifty-seven years old, he was certainly fit and looked younger than his years. Everyone hung their cameras round his neck and wishing him luck, we left him looking more like an American tourist than an intrepid trekker.

The next few hours were the worst of the whole trek, an utter nightmare. I was so exhausted that I lagged behind the others finding it impossible to keep to their pace. The blizzard reduced the visibility to a couple of yards and froze as it covered the path. I called out to the others but they did not hear me. All I could do was carry on blindly in the approximate direction I had been going. I kept slipping and falling, my back was in agony. I was utterly miserable; I had no idea where I was. I could only hope that someone would realize that I was missing and come and look for me. Then out of the snow Pemba appeared I was safe at last. I discovered much later that Kristi had realized that I was no longer with them and had sent Pemba back to look for me.

I stumbled in camp at 4pm and climbing into my tent, I was offered brandy by my tent mate Valerie. Never was anything more welcome. That night I could not eat my supper and just about managed some soup. This caused consternation amongst the others who thought I must be nearing my end to refuse food. My appetite was normally enormous; I wasn't called the dustbin for nothing. Tired out and happy my tears dried and fear forgotten, I realized that I had accomplished my ambition. In spite of the odds, I had trekked to Everest and had climbed higher than second camp.

Day 17.
MONDAY APRIL 18 1977
LOBUJE/PANGBOCHE 13,000 feet (7 hours approx)

After sleeping the sleep of the dead, I woke up refreshed and found the snow was six inches deep outside and the thermometer registered -19 degrees C, the coldest night of the trip beating our earlier record of -15 degrees C. My wet boots had frozen solid and were difficult to put on over the plastic bags which I had put on my feet to keep them dry. I did not fancy wet socks once the boots began to thaw. Who knows I might even get trench foot. Heaven forbid!

Snow blindness was the 'Illness of the Day,' Pemba suffered badly as he had not worn his sunglasses yesterday. The porters were affected and I felt sorry for the little Sherpani girls who could hardly see at all. All our spare sun specs were doled out and Pam improvised some emergency ones from cardboard and string.

At the top of the pass, we had a game of snowballs; everyone had recovered their spirits now that we had left Lobuje.

We decided to ambush the Thomas Cooke group, but when we learnt from the remnants of the party that we just missed them, we felt we could hardly attack them with snowballs; as sickness had taken its toll of the group. One of them riding on a yak looked pathetic. We felt infinitely superior. At least we were all on our feet. We really were mean about them.

Lunch was scheduled at Pheriche; by then my boots were sopping wet however my socks were dry. The plastic bags had proved to be an inspiration. Today's walking was easy as it was all downwards.

Pheriche is a popular stop for trekkers and climbers. There is a rudimentary hospital in Pheriche that is operated under the auspices of the Himalayan Rescue Association which is headquartered in Kathmandu. The Pheriche hospital is open only during the two trekking/climbing seasons. Although the hospital was built with Japanese assistance in 1975, it is staffed by Nepalis and volunteer physicians who are mostly from the USA, Europe, Canada and Australia. Pheriche was primarily a farming village raising potatoes and buckwheat, and keeping yaks. However, now in the summer many of its men are employed by trekkers as guides and bearers.

The village was hopefully pandering to the tourists with roughly scrawled notices advertising the delights of the two 'hotels.' It felt like the height of civilization. Ailsa was there to greet us, fully recovered from her altitude sickness. She looked remarkably clean as she had been living the life of comparative luxury while we were up in the frozen wastes; sleeping in a proper bed and washing every day! She was civilized and polite after having been away from us for a couple of days and appalled at the deterioration in our table manners.

When we arrived in Pangboche in the late afternoon, the mist surrounded us, chilling us to the bone. This large village was laid out on terraces and had its own *gompa* which housed the famous Yeti relics of a shriveled hand and head. As there was no sign of Gerard and Lapka we decided to go and visit the *gompa* without them. The monk who showed us round had an eye for profit and tried to charge us for everything we looked at. We agree to pay two rupees each to view the relics but declined his offer of five rupees a head to go and see the monks' quarters. Custom dictates we leave our boots outside the main door of the *gompa,* when we came out we found the Sherpanis had played a joke on us and had muddled them all up. We had an awful job sorting them out.

We descended through the cobbled streets between the houses to our field to find the tents up. We were thankful of the shelter of our homes and a cup of tea as the wind had picked up and the temperature had dropped. I hoped it would be warmer tonight at least it was not snowing. Unfortunately the weather stopped us visiting the Hillary School at Pangboche.

There was a sudden shout from one of the Sherpas. Gerard and Lapka were coming in the distance. We were so happy to see them safe and to hear an account of their adventures. Gerard had climbed to the top of Kalapatar although he found it slippery with the ice and snow which was then melting in the sun. He had thought it worthwhile because the weather had stayed fine and view from the top was magnificent. The night at Gorakshep had not been too uncomfortable as he had been invited to share a tent with some New Zealanders, preferable to the hotel. Our 'Man about Town' was feted and toasted for his fortitude and endurance.

What a day!

Yeti skull and hand at Pangboche

Day 18.
TUESDAY APRIL 19 1977
PANGBOCHE/SYANGBOCHE   13,000
feet (6 hours approx)

This was our last day and I was full of mixed feelings, happy to be finishing the trek because of exhaustion. I have suffered a lack of energy since that dreadful day from Gorakshep to Lobuje, yet I was sad that the journey was nearly over.

The climb upwards was steep and the sun blazed down on us. Soon we were stopping for rests, just so that we would see our magnificent snowcapped mountains one last time. They had been our constant companions and friends during the past weeks. Will we ever see this dazzling panorama again?

We were off again to visit our last Hillary School, a Hindu school teacher, disillusioned with trying to teach Buddhist children and alone in this community, who was thinking of giving up and returning to Kathmandu to be with his own people. Through an interpreter we found out that he had few visitors to the school but he cheered up when we made an appearance and also with the gifts we brought. He said we had given him fresh hope. At last somebody cared and he was no longer forgotten. We were moved by our reception.

We heard that the distinguished artist Kappa Kalden Sherpa famous for his murals in Tengboche Monastery was to bring some of his pictures to the local hospital in the evening for us to see. Although we waited we were disappointed because he didn't turn up. Hopefully we might see the pictures tomorrow at the airstrip.

We were given a short tour of the hospital by the doctor-in-charge who is from New Zealand. He told us stories about his hospital and how the patients always insist on him joining them for a drink of *rakshi.* Because it is rude to refuse he had to resort to all sorts of subterfuges to drink only a token toast with them. Toni suddenly produced a bottle of whiskey from her bag and presented it to the doctor. Gerard called back later and helped him drink it. I was jealous when I heard this but remained silent. We donated our excess medicines and toilet rolls to the hospital.

Gerard me Marilyn and Ed

Supper or rather dinner was a sumptuous affair. Chatuman had prepared a special meal of all our favourite dishes, soup, potatoes with their jackets, Sherpa chutney (chilli with tomatoes) and stuffed potato torpedoes filled with egg and butter followed by cheese and biscuits. Food was short in this area of the Solu Khumbu and we admired his ingenuity in producing such a delicious meal.

The campfire, our last, was a happy affair with lots of *chang* and songs. The Sherpas taught us some of their dances and to my delight everyone got up and joined in. No-one wanted to go to bed so we stayed up until all hours. The party was a grand finale to our trek.

Day 19.
WEDNESDAY APRIL 20 1977
SYANGBOCHE/KATHMANDU via LUKLA

The camp site so dreary last night has been transformed this morning by the sun rising up behind the icy peaks. As we sipped our last bed tea we gazed just one more time at the mountains in all their glory that have come to say goodbye to us. We have done our final pack; our kitbags are much lighter as we have given most of our gear to the Sherpas and porters, I donated mine to the Sherpanis who always seem to get left out of the perks and work just as hard. Our last breakfast was cornflakes, omelets and mugs of sweet smoke flavoured tea.

We had to go and within the hour we had arrived at the Syangboche airstrip, to find that all the trekkers in the Solukhumbu seem to have had the same idea and were deciding to leave at the same time. The tourists from the Hotel Everest View will get priority as they are on an organized tour and the airstrip belongs to the hotel.

The last photographs have been taken; Pemba has presented each one of us with a *katak* as we made our last farewells to the Sherpas and the porters who have become our friends.

Rumours and counter rumours are flying round that the flights will be cancelled again today because of the weather. Two independent trekkers, who had regaled me at Lobuje with stories of roast chicken and hot showers in their hostel, decided they couldn't be bothered to wait so off they trekked to Lukla and from there hoped to fly to Kathmandu. I was tempted to go with them but Pam has now discovered we will be flown out first. Bales Tours seem to always get priority everywhere they go.

The place suddenly went mad; pictures were bought at outrageous prices from Kappa Kalden Sherpa; Gerard spends another hundred dollars on souvenirs he could have bought in Kathmandu for much less. However with his business acumen he will probably get at least twice his money back on resale.

Pam calls 'Six' and off we ran to the six-seater Pilatus Porter plane waiting on the grass. I had forgotten my umbrella again and Thondup hands it to me and as I raced, the pilot yells,

'Get out, I can take only five.'

I got out of the plane and once again I was told to get back in again. Finally off we go to Lukla where a Sirdar friend of Pemba took care of us and put us on a Twin Otter plane minus our kitbags bound for Kathmandu. They were left on the Syangboche airstrip. Later on they were brought out from Nepal by the Thomas Cooke group and mine was delivered to my home a week after I had returned to the UK.

Flying over the mountains for the last time, I wondered how long I would be able to keep Everest with me and how long would it take before I can make a journey like this again. We landed at Kathmandu and as the trek slid into the past I was left with a deep satisfaction that despite the odds stacked against me I had achieved my goal.

PS An abridged version of *Everest or Bust* was published in *The People* magazine in 1978.

Epilogue

We had a reunion at Valerie's house. After that Kristi who was originally from Zimbabwe went back there. Gerard returned to Brazil and sent me some amethyst quartsz which is still in my possession. I remained a friend of Ailsa who continued to work at the Scott Polar Institute Cambridge until her retirement. About five years ago she became ill and I have not heard from her or any of the others since.

L'envoi

We are the Pilgrims master; we shall go
Always a little further; it may be
Beyond that last blue mountain barred with snow

BALES TOURS GROUP KATHMANDU
Back Row left to right
David, ? Terry, Doris, Ailsa,
Norman ? Valerie, me

Front Row left to right
Pemba, Gerard, Dolly, Pam, Toni?
Sherpani, Kristi

Suggested Packing List
(If you are thinking of going to Everest)

The following weight restrictions apply to the internal flights within your itinerary:
Phaplu-Kathmandu-Lukla
15kg Hold baggage, 5kg Hand baggage
Left luggage can be left in Kathmandu

You Must Bring the Following Items
Hiking boots (or approach type trainers) – waterproof
Sandals for river crossings (just in case)
Socks
Trekking type windproof Waterproof overtrousers
Underwear
Casual shirt and/or T-shirts
Fleece jacket or warm jumper
Waterproof jacket
Sunhat
Warm hat
Sunglasses
Gloves or mittens

Head torch and spare batteries
Sun protection (including total bloc for lips, nose etc.)
Water bottles 1 litre x2
Washbag and toiletries
Antibacterial handwash
Small towel
Toilet Roll
Sleeping bag (comfort rated -5°C)*
Warm jacket (down) (we hire one for you in Kathmandu)
Basic First Aid Kit including: antiseptic cream, throat lozenges,
diarrhoea treatment (Imodium), altitude (Diamox), painkillers,
plasters and blister treatment, insect repellent, and rehydration salts (Dioralite),
Antibiotics such as Amoxcyillin (Chest), Ciprofloxacin (Intestines)

The symptoms of altitude sickness include:
A throbbing headache that usually gets worse during the night and when
you wake up.

Lack of appetite.

Feeling sick to your stomach.

You may vomit.

Feeling weak and tired.

Waking up during the night and not sleeping well.

Feeling dizzy.

Legs swell with fluid retention.

Kidneys do not work properly.

Acetazolamide (Diamox) may be prescribed to hasten acclimatization.

Acetazolamide is a diuretic (a drug that increases urine output) that increases kidney excretion of bicarbonate. This decreases the blood pH, thereby stimulating extra breathing, which results in higher oxygen levels in the blood.

In addition, acetazolamide corrects night time pauses in breathing known as periodic breathing. Acetazolamide also improves symptoms of insomnia. This medication may also be utilized in a preventative manner in people with a prior history of altitude sickness.

Additional (but a good idea)

Thermal baselayer - leggings
Sleeping bag liner
Scarf or face mask (handy if dust is in the air)
Camera
Repair kit – (eg. needle, thread, duct tape)
Power bank for re-charging your camera, Kindle and phone
Kendal mint cake and sweets
A diary and pens
Some presents like pens or crayons for visiting schools

Etiquette in Lodges & Tea Houses

1. No noise as walls may be thin.
2. Do not enter kitchen unless invited to do so
3. Respect the privacy of the owners as it is probably their home too

4. No haggling the higher you get the dearer and more basic it becomes and it causes offence.

5. Change shoes in the house

Prayer flags in the wind

SOME BIRDS FOUND IN THE EVEREST REGION

Bearded Vulture

Blood Pheasant

Fire-tailed Myzornis

GoldenEagle

117

Grandala

Himalayan Monal

Himalayan Snowcock

HimalayanVulture

Red Crossbill

SatyrTragopan

Scarlet Finch

SnowPartridge

Snow Pigeons

SpottedLaughingthrush

Tibetan Siskin

TibetanSnowcock

Map Giving General Idea Of Our Trek

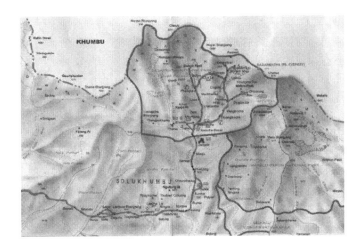

Map is dated 2017 and gives only a rough idea of our trek. Phaplu not shown is to the left of the route

My Trekking Pass

Hindu idol Kathmandu

Hindu Shrine Kathmandu

Acknowledgements

Bonington, Chris, *Everest the Hard Way 1976,* Arrow Books UK 1977

Denman, Earl, *Alone to Everest 1954,* The Travel Book Club London

Donaldson, Jean, *Innocents to Everest 1976,* United Writers Publications Cornwall

Fleming, Robert L, Fleming, Robert L. Junior & Bangdel Lain Singh, *Birds of Nepal,* Private Publication Kathmandu

Grahame, Iain, *Blood Pheasant,* The Mitre Press London c1972

Hayes, John L. *Trekking in Mt Everest and Solu Khumbu 1975,* Avalok Publishers Distributors Kathmandu

Hillary, Edmund, *Nothing Venture, Nothing Win 1975,* Hodder & Stoughton, London Auckland Sydney Toronto

Hillary, Sir Edmund, *Schoolhouse in the Clouds 1964,* Quality Book Club Edition

Hillary, Louise, *High Time 1973,* Hodder & Stoughton London Auckland Sydney Toronto

Hunt, John, *Ascent of Everest 1954,* The Reprint Society London

Ramsey Ullman, James, *Man on Everest 1955,* The Reprint Society London

Steele, Peter, *Doctor on Everest 1972,* Readers Union Newton Abbott 1973

von Furer-Haimendorf, Christoph, *Himalayan Traders 1975,* John Murray London

Younghusband, Sir Francis, *The Epic of Mount Everest 1926,* Edward Arnold & Co London

Wikipedia and other media sources

Photographs by Eileen Hewson FRGS and other members of the group

About the Author

Eileen Hewson FRGS

Eileen Hewson FRGS has been travelling to the remote areas of the Himalaya for over 40 years.

Her travels have taken her to Everest and Nepal, along the Karakorum Highway between Pakistan & China, Bhutan, Pakistan, Sikkim, Darjeeling, Kashmir, Ladakh & Zanskar and many others. Her plans for the future include the newly opened Kingdom of Mustang and Eastern Bhutan. She still talks about her trek to Everest. See www.himalayanmiscellany.com

Her inspiration was the late explorer and writer Michel Peissel who travelled to these places in the 1960's and 70's.

For many years Eileen's concern for with the fate of old graveyards in Ireland and Asia inspired her to document many of the inscriptions. Her searches took her to India, the Himalayas and Sri Lanka (Ceylon) where she surveyed many European burial grounds. Finding an Irish heritage in the Falklands was a surprise so it was recorded before it disappeared.

The results are published by The Kabristan Archives and are available to the general public at a nominal price at www.kabristanbookshop.com.

She has a blog, see www.genealogysrilanka.com which allows the public to post their Sri Lankan Genealogy queries for free.

Eileen is the author of over 100 publications, a Fellow of the Royal Geographical Society and a member of the British Association of Cemeteries in South Asia (BACSA.)

28234475R00078

Printed in Poland
by Amazon Fulfillment
Poland Sp. z o.o., Wrocław